Who Likes the Sun?

Written by
Etta Kaner

Illustrated by
Marie Lafrance

Kids Can Press

Who likes the sun?

I like the sun because
it warms me up.

I do!

I wonder how the sun warms me when it's so far away.

These rays warm you even after they travel about 150 million kilometers (93 million miles) to get to Earth.

The sun is a giant ball of fire. It is *very* hot. Its surface is about 55 times hotter than boiling water.

The sun sends out very strong rays of heat and light.

I like the sun because
it melts icicles.

I wonder how
icicles are made.

Then the sun melts more snow.
Water drops drip down the
icicle to its tip.

They freeze when it turns cold again.
The icicle gets bigger and bigger.

An icicle starts when the sun melts snow into water. Water drops drip down.

When it gets cold enough, the water drops freeze.

I like the sun because I
get to wear my sunglasses.

I wonder how sunglasses work.

Sunglasses are like sunscreen. Their special glass stops the sun's rays from burning your eyes.

Their dark color helps shade your eyes so you don't squint.

Sunlight is very strong. Just as your skin can be sunburned, so can your eyes.

I like the sun because it helps dry the grass after a rain.

I wonder where
dew comes from.

Grass and spiderwebs are cool at night.
That's why you see dew on them in
the morning.

I wonder where
the water goes.

The water vapor becomes part of the air.

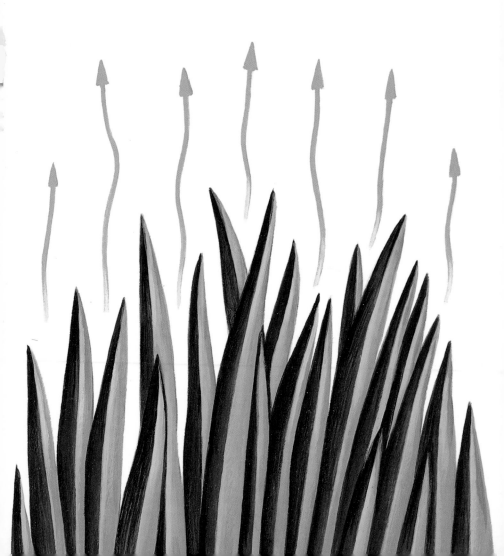

When the sun comes out, it heats the water on the grass.

The heated water turns into very tiny drops of water called vapor.

I like the sun because it
makes dewdrops glow.

The evening air just above the ground has water vapor in it.

The water vapor changes to water drops when it touches something cool. These water drops are called dew.

I like the sun because I can play shadow tag.

I wonder why I
have a shadow.

When the sun is low in the sky, your shadow is long.

You have a shadow when your body blocks sunlight from reaching the ground. This happens because the sun can't shine through you.

When the sun is high
in the sky, your
shadow is short.

I like the sun because it turns grapes into raisins.

I wonder how grapes
turn into raisins.

When this happens, the grapes shrink.

It takes about three weeks for a grape to shrink into a raisin.

Grapes are picked when they are juicy and sweet.

Then they are put on trays to dry in the sun. The heat of the sun makes the water in the grapes go out into the air.

I like the sun because
it helps flowers grow.

I wonder why some flowers have a smell and others don't.

Other flowers attract insects by their colors. They don't need a smell to attract insects.

Some flowers have a smell to attract insects. Insects help flowers make seeds. Flowers make seeds to grow more plants.

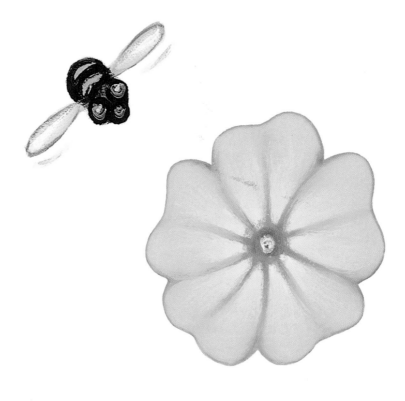

I like the sun because it makes water sparkle.

I wonder why the water sparkles.

When there are lots of waves reflecting light, the water looks sparkly.

Water sparkles when it has little waves.

Each wave acts like a mirror. When sunlight hits a wave, the light bounces off it. The water is reflecting the sunlight.

I like the sun because
it makes rainbows.

I wonder how the sun makes rainbows.

When the sun shines through them,
its white light splits into the different
colors to make a rainbow.

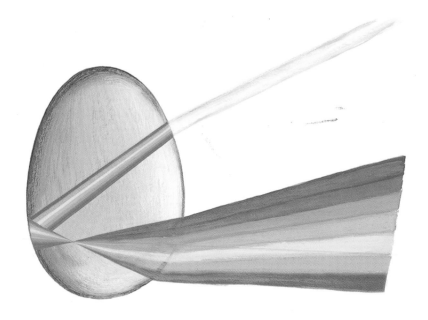

Sunlight has all the colors of a rainbow in it — red, orange, yellow, green, blue, indigo and violet. All the colors mixed together make white light. This is the daylight we usually see.

After a rain, there are water drops in the air.

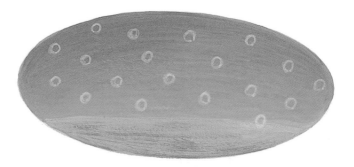

I like the sun because it makes the sky look beautiful in the evening.

I wonder why the sky
sometimes turns red.

The blue in sunlight scatters all over the sky. This makes the sky look blue during the day.

As the sun sets, blue light scatters even more. It scatters so much that it disappears. Only the redder part of the sunlight is left for you to see.

Sunlight travels through a layer of dust, air and clouds to reach us. This layer is called atmosphere.

As sunlight travels, some of its colors bounce off bits of dust and air in the atmosphere. This scatters the colors.

I like the sun because I can play outside during the day.

I wonder where the
sun goes at night.

When the sun shines on your side of
Earth, it's day.

When your side is turned away from
the sun, it's night. Good night!

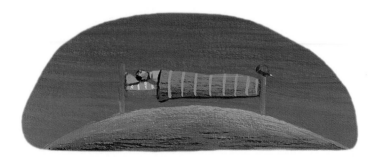

The sun never moves. It is always in the same spot in the sky.

But Earth, with you on it, is always turning. This is why the sun shines on different parts of Earth at different times.

Why do *you* like the sun?